Lectio Violant

Steve Ely

Lectio Violant

Shearsman Books

First published in the United Kingdom in 2021 by
Shearsman Books Ltd
PO Box 4239
Swindon
SN3 9FN

Shearsman Books Ltd Registered Office
30–31 St. James Place, Mangotsfield, Bristol BS16 9JB
(this address not for correspondence)

www.shearsman.com

ISBN 978-1-84861-754-4

Copyright © Steve Ely, 2021.

The right of Steve Ely to be identified as the author
of this work has been asserted by him in accordance with the
Copyrights, Designs and Patents Act of 1988.
All rights reserved.

Acknowledgements
Some of the poems in this book were first published in the following
journals, magazines and websites:
The Dark Horse, *The High Window*, *The London Review of Books*,
The Manhattan Review, *The Poetry Review*, *Poetry Salzburg Review*,
Stand Magazine and *Strix*.

The final sequence was published as a pamphlet
by *New Walk Editions*.

Thanks to Ed Reiss for his comments on the typescript,
which helped improve a number of poems and clarify a thing or two.

Cover image by the author.

CONTENTS

Sufficient vnto the day
Improvisations on Matthew VI

Treasures of heauen and earth	11
Theeues breake thorow	12
Where your treasure is, there will your heart be also	13
Thy whole body shalbe full of light	14
How great is that darkenesse	15
No man can serve two masters	16
Take no thought for your life	17
The foules of the aire	18
The lillies of the field	19
Solomon in all his glory	20
Yee of little faith	21
The kingdome of God, and his righteousnesse	22
Sufficient vnto the day is the euill thereof	23

The countrey of the Gadarenes
Improvisations on Mark V

The countrey of the Gadarenes	27
No man could bind them	28
Jesus afarre off	29
A great herd of swine, feeding	30
Publish in Decapolis	31
All men did marueille	32
Had suffered many things, of many Physicians	33
Vertue had gone out of him	34
Be not afraid, onley believe	35
Why make ye this adoe, and weepe?	36
The damosell is not dead, but sleepeth	37
Talitha cumi	38
Some thing should be given her to eate	39

Ioy in the presence of the Angels of God
Improvisations on Luke XV

Publicanes and sinners	43
Murmured, murmured	44
This man receiueth sinners	46
Ninety nine in the wilderness	48
No repentance	51
Reioyce	52
Ioy in the presence of the Angels of God	54
A farre country	55
The huskes that the swine did eate	56
No man gaue vnto him	58
I have sinned against heauen	59
Fell on his necke	60
The fatted calfe	61

I beheld Satan as lightning fall from heauen
An improvisation on Luke X

Exsultet	65
The Feather of Ma'at	66
The Mother of Naim	67
Tarshish	68
Ego te absolvo	69
The Passing of Joel Theriot	70
I beheld Satan as lightning fall from heauen	71
A Dog Speculates on the Mind of Newton	72
Goe, and do thou likewise	74
Ecce Homo	76
Capernaum	77
Melencolia, I	78
Hæc nox est	79
Notes	82

Sufficient vnto the day

Improvisations on Matthew VI

Treasures of heauen and earth

Das große Rasenstück, Albrecht Dürer.

Turf smocked in fodder; cock's foot,
bent, smooth meadow. Flushed
bruisewort crewelling, pee-beds
stitched in gold. Bird's-eye blinks
from rumpled bedstraw, milfoil
boa'd in plumes. Blood-starred
hound's-tongue, slobbery, hackled,
decocted pox bane, cool rich piss.
Sod wick with scrabs. Odalisque
cow mouth cropping and drooling,
back-ended in tit milk, splattering pats.

Theeues breake thorow

There is the dove, and there is the serpent.

Milky Bathsheba, buttocks erect,
soaping her glory in dew-drenched
windflowers: David tearing his Psalter
from deep rhododendrons.
Perulae wilting, dript confetti;
roding woodcock, vespertine
thrumming of bees. Full beam Venus
driving out drones, Mars riddancing
maids from the rides. Bedded in bracken
with bot flies biting, creamy arse
crack, clocked, cockchafered,
stagged in lines, rohypnol.

Where your treasure is, there will your heart be also

A buxom wench, firm-fleshed, strong-shouldered and smooth skinned.

White flesh split to star-pipped heart.
Found blade unfallen silver.
Skinnydip bob-fest; Adam's pearmain,
ribstoned Eve. God's brandished
burrknot, serpent pitching
bloody ploughman. Flesh
burkha'd in fig leaves and rotting
to dust. Jobs burdened with billions,
sick with canker. Good works
building credit in heaven,
heaven from ploughman's earth:
Al-Raqqa, Brasilia, the City.
Kids scrumping catsheads,
Nancy Jackson—*those were the days!*—
before Apple Garth and Orchard View,
live paedosex on iPhones.

Thy whole body shalbe full of light

One sharing shack with jays
and leverets, honey hived
in walls. Hearth-rug goat kid,
fetlock splinted, slow worm coiled
in coals. Swifts dip the lintel,
antswarm trawling, henbane herb garth
wick with greens. Gate unhinged
and damp grass trampled, danced
the quaking fields—with Angels,
star-sown, dark earth fallen, scythe-
winged rising, quick with screams.

How great is that darkenesse

Ring road glazed in lights.
Buffering macula, dampened panes;
muted YouTube central heating.
Cold coffee and donuts,
gastro-oesophageal reflux.
The heart's a torn-up map, voyaging
blind through doldrum darkness.
Through muffling glass
high greylags trumpet,
skeining wild and north.

No man can serve two masters

Walking that kelp-wrecked,
Hesperidean strand, notes
sanderling, turnstone, purple sand.
Shags hard and low across the surf swell,
crab boat's outboard drone. Hauled pots
and crates and nylon holdalls,
pagurus, AKs, shrinkwrapped keys,
the freedom of the golden isle
where phalaropes flirt
and red-throats flume and wail.

Take no thought for your life

Meanwhile at the Spahn movie ranch
Charlie is strumming
we are stardust we are golden
as Banksy stencils in pregnant blood
piggies piggies political piggies
he catwalked the Haight like a Levite
but Tex was tossing squares
from the pinnacle of the temple
and L. Ron Hubbard spitting Hollywood longpork
Charlie called the whole thing fugazy
it aint bread brother
but every word that proceedeth.

The foules of the aire

The peregrines of Drax
hunt nightjars under floodlights;
in her cooling tower eyrie,
falcon broods midst litterèd skulls.
Tiercel on the gantry, retching
and preening: screaming hypo-
glycaemia fires him aloft; narcotic
bloodsugars sate him to sleep.
Sun flares and dies. Moths
blottering the nimbus. Blurs
scything from darkness smash
and explode; body down,
feathery antennae. Biomass
cast in the furnace.

The lillies of the field

Fumaria officinalis

Earthsmoke cure my adjust humours,
sore disordered heart; for scabbed am I
and foully tettered, fluxed with gleets
and weeping. Wax doll greencorn
flopped and rolled, breast-cropt
squeazing milk. Hard heads thumbed-off,
wild splay-winged beating—for sin
and burning. The Law of the Lord.
The grass of the field. The song of the turtle.

Solomon in all his glory

The reptile brain parades its secret:
our flesh is grass for burning.
Somme's dutiful slaughter,
the gulags of Shirebrook and Laos.
Meanwhile in Steve Jobs' perfumed gardens,
the Goat of Mendes mainlines vril.
Marilyn fuckt with chainsaws.
Sting strums his golden lute.

Yee of little faith

Scissored-off heads of gaping pratensis,
baled in shrinkwrapped haylage;
perdix bleeds in crewcut rye.
Farmhands snapping at the five bar gate,
dropping crusts and fist-crushed foil.
Ratchet laughter and DJ prattle
rattle through the hedgerow—goatish
peering through may's smashed lattice,
an orchard of soft-trunked elders;
nannies aloft in florescent sambucus,
billies rutting and ripping the vernal.
Pipe and tabor sound from street,
clogs clattering the camber—*alle
manere men, the mene and the rich,
worchyng and wandrying*—jynx
pursing her lips through a grass blade.

The kingdome of God, and his righteousnesse

Depression is rage turned inward.

The one failing to decapitate
the get-orf-my-land equestrian
out riding with her daughter, also failed
to gibbet the kite-killing keeper
and gouge out the eyes of the Ofsted inspector,
so servile in his shame: but if the prisons
were full, the need would be less
and the Lord would come riding
the thermidor of heaven,
his fissile stars like glinting pangas,
our good black writhing holes.

Sufficient vnto the day is the euill thereof

Three days and nights I roamed
the oak groves, quick with henbane,
pillicocked raw with love.
I coupled with she-wolves and tied
in their traps, by the beck
I gropecunted naiads. Did I rise
with the pern from combes of sweet Earth,
to ruddy Arcturus, the microhertz
whispers of Yuggoth? The aeons
shoaled like herring and bled
from the nets; cuneiform beebuzz
deciphered to laughter. And pale
as a parsnip I woke in my plots
to the guffawings of my neighbour—
a man on a ladder, re-adjusting his dish,
that he might receive his signal.

The countrey of the Gadarenes

Improvisations on Mark V

The countrey of the Gadarenes

How they feed, those that feed the swine:
tongues of larks and peacock semen,
clits of dollshead damsels. Pigs in blankets,
shanked and scratching, popped like corks
beneath the corkscrew tail. Rinse the filth
with lapped champagne, bruised members
soothe in tart saliva. Revived in DMT,
Viagra, proud years pass in a single day;
but for those that cry on the unbound
mountain, teeth gnawed blunt on stones,
each hour's a day, and every day, a lifetime.
Delivered unto drowning, sparing cities
from their rage; where sow-papped MILFs
and nymphet piglings split the vomitorium:
send vs the swine, that we may enter into them.

No man could bind them

No man could bind him, so he had to be killed.
He'd been recusing himself from maintaining
his stretch of the turnpike, over which he'd hover
in his lawnmower-engined flying-machine.
His feet never touched the municipal earth.
He potshotted bailiffs, the Sheriff and Lord Lieutenant;
so far so good—set the dogs on the gasman,
put a Rambo knife through young Ben Dyker's ball.
When the County ordered A and the Commune
countered B, he waved a shotgun Magna Carta
and told them—*See?* So the County raised the militia
and the Commune rode the night. He took a few with him,
but they purged him from the lists. The incomers
turned out decent types: they mend their road,
return Ben's ball, seem keen to learn our AB—*See?*

Jesus afarre off

*If any man loue not the Lord Iesus Christ, let him
bee anathema. Maranatha!*

Once, nesting for woodcock in Bent Plantation,
I thought I caught a glimpse of him, escaping
through the trees. Maybe I chased after him,
and maybe he did look down on me, from the top
of that embankment—in blouson rouge, indeterminate
Sta-Prest jeans. But truly the mother bird exploded
before a jury of my peers, three damp and trembling
chicks exposed by our boots in a bowl of unzipped
eggshells. The fourth clutched tight between her thighs,
she crashed in bracken at the foot of the slope,
where Trampas took her on the snatched half-volley;
and where I gathered the bleating peep and him restored
to his orphaned siblings, the absent father's care.
We marked the nest with a plastic sack, found
bright red snagged in the raking hawthorns' gloom.
And flew it like a flag, hidden in plain sight, the key
to our moocher's map: five fence posts to the East,
four hawthorns to the South; where three days later,
we almost certainly never found them, alive
with maggots in their little depression.

A great herd of swine, feeding

The nicest man in the world is turning the crank
of the grinder. His wife, the nicest woman
in the world, shovels in the meat; a brace
of garefowl, thirty billion passenger pigeons,
inexhaustible centillions of wren. The mince curls
into the mixing bowl, where the nicest boys and girls
in the world form it into patties; tofu, MacBooks,
All-Inclusive. Beneath the bowl, the nicest dogs
and cats in the world are licking up the scraps;
indenture, asylum, hope. The nicest kings and queens
in the world and the worstest James Bond villains
have befriended us on Facebook, posting and sharing,
updating their status; the most radical poets
and prophets of the day heckle with fierce emojis,
winning spoil of likes and OBEs. And the nicest, best
socialised, most caring children in the epochal
history of the sapiential race, are concerned to wear
fashionable garments of meat, rendered from stem cells
of glaucous macaws in the wombs of 3D printers.
And the slender-billed curlew and jenny wren sing,

O Hitler, O Truman, O Djugashvili,
O Marburg, Ebola, Lord Jesus come.

Publish in Decapolis

His starry compassion was slaughterer's zeal
for the Kingdom of the Poor. Pigs and demons,
unclean spirits; metaphors, displacements.
An issue of blood twelve years—ten thousand plus
and counting. The Baptist's head on a charger,
a just and holy man; Gandhi, Torres, Dedan
Kimathi. The Assyrian King List, Tudiya
to Merkel and May. How shalwe be whole
when the opulent break us with hunger and lash?
The meek arm themselves from their cutlery drawers
and lunge from under their skirts; incipit Vespasian,
the razing of the Temple. Tell it on Wall Street,
proclaim it in Pudong: a starre out of Jacob
and a Scepter from Israel, marching in his Way;
linked arms and clenched fists, darkweb ordnance
from Krajina and Sevastopol, divisions of the Pope.

All men did marueille

All men did marueille at the coming of the Christ,
his signs and wonders; the healing of the Beast,
the rebirth of Kahless, the life-changing flimflam
of Weightwatchers, Anthony Robbins. On his farm
he raised skunk and played the gee-tar, hit Main Street
on weekends to brawl with the sheriffs and shoot up
City Hall's snake-oil men. The scrapes he got into
and out of—*my stars!*—some said he was a god.

They asked him to set them free: so he made them
his slaves; they asked him to set them free: he said
free your goddamn selves; they asked him to set them free:
and he taught them in parables; they asked him
to set them free: so he killed them all, or something:
who the fuck knows how shit like this plays out?

Had suffered many things, of many Physicians

Since the fall our seed has been punished
to the fifth generation. No future but scraps
from the banqueters' table or leaving the dead
to bury the dead and joining their killers.

So uncap the shaft and layer us down,
like captured carbon, or radioactive carbon rods,
stacked floor-to-roof on the maingate rip
in spongy pillars like badly maintained chocks.

Vertue had gone out of him

Royd's saturate furrows are bleeding from sunset,
long pigs cooling in the squall's bright lee; where
his boots are clubs of earth, his trousers plastered
and the folds of his ripstop running like gullies
as he hurdles the drills, earth sucking and collapsing
under his gait, shouts cracking like rifles
and tractors trundling their beelines behind him;
where he had no weapon, and at that moment
wanted no war, yet nevertheless feared
that he might kill, and therefore anxious,
with buckling at the knees and tightening
across the chest; but mostly for his greyhounds,
careless of shotguns and the French king's serjeants,
bounding around him with puzzlement and with joy.

Be not afraid, onley believe

*Until one is committed, there is hesitancy, the chance to
draw back [...] the moment one definitely commits oneself,
then Providence moves too.*

Threw down his pen and took up his Active Hydroponic
Growing System, belendek, dwale and datura;
Freya's Day, Satyr's Day, Sun. Who is like unto the Beast?
And who is able to make warre with him? Me,
a mouth to speak great things, to blaspheme his Name,
his tabernacle, his wife and kids in his DNA's sacred
muniment room. Threw down his Active Hydroponic
Growing System to take up the gun and O what fun
to see them run, and die their seed, in story O;
threw down his gun and erected scaffolds, dug pits,
raised altars to Great Cernunnos; threw down Bastilles,
freeing some to slaughter and slaughtering others;
so the land gave up its bounty, and rivers were milk
and lakes were ale and copshops tiled in custards;
threw down the withered machinery of state, and broadcast
belendek, dwale and datura, our bared souls sailing
from Ravenser Odd for Cockayne and the Akashic record.

Why make ye this adoe, and weepe?

What country can preserve its liberties if their rulers are not warned from time to time that their people preserve the spirit of resistance? Let them take arms. [...] The tree of liberty must be refreshed from time to time with the blood of patriots and tyrants. It is its natural manure.

Here's the Queen shaking hands with Martin McGuinness,
once, twice, thrice: she's still alive; unlike Paisley,
or Nelson Mandela, embracing de Klerk going up
for their Nobel Prize. Liz Blakelock, whisked off her feet
by Winnie at the Notting Hill Carnival, calypso
smiles from under his dented helmet; the Six
playing gin with Denning. War by other means;
peace at any cost? The law and the courts and the cops
and Her Majesty's Forces. Bill Gates v Karen Matthews.
It's a wonderful life, and the price is always murder,
if you can call it that, when the Monster lashes out
at Frankenstein or the lab-chimp brains the electrode-
inserting researcher. *Don't jump!* little odd body says:
prise cobbles from the street, brandish your pitchfork,
smuggle Libyan RPGs; touch life, manure the tree.

The damosell is not dead, but sleepeth

Low ruin, enclosed in a copse of planted Georgian trees;
shorn common drilled with wheat and rape, where ploughshares
grind on sunken ashlar, shear skulls and expose femurs.
Shattered dynasties glint from tilth, Latimer, Mowbray,
Foliot, Zouch, the arms of Gaunt, Black Prince and York.
What brought these High and Mighty here, to the chapel
below the limestone crag, twixt Hangmanstone
and Ludwell Hill, overlooking the ings to Dearne?
St. Elen's spring, the gushing omphalos of this flood-gouged
scarp since the pre-arboreal Holocene; back-filled now
and drained to ditch, her violated temenos strewn
with field-walked votive scatter; flakes of Mesolithic chert,
burnt Beaker flint and Bronze Age spearheads, Samian,
Grey ware, Coalfield White. Here ceorls processed in garlands
to the beat of beer and drum, and under quick at Lady's cave
made Mass, destroyed their silver; broke war-blades out of use.

Subinfeudate chaos of tenure: Cresacre of Newmarche
of Warenne of the King—Henry, the Bastard's fourth-born,
in whose reign rose the altar on another usurper's bones:
the chapel of St. Helen, to the glory of bishop and king.
But the locals were prone to dropping their aitches,
and though her earth was torn from them, onoured their Lady,
with Masses and branches of hard-berried quick, trespass,
coursing, Actual Bodily Harm ... wavy-dissolve from England
's dreaming to the Coach and Horses car park, St. Peter
chiming chuck-out time some disco Saturday night.
A couple in their cups, some latter-day Alice and Percy perhaps,
giggle the street and moonlit stubbles to bed among bales
by the copse off Helen's Lane: where they woke
to freezing dew and wraith-mist, rose of fingering dawn,
ragged apparitions of the chapel's White Lady,
haunting our dreaming from Elicon, Ludwell Hill.

Talitha cumi

From the sump of the sink of the backstreet terrace,
the celebrity surgeon's sharp bin; the panic of one
who could've, who should've [...] stainless steel, tissue
and scraping, flushed, disposal; I know, I knew;
smothercate fish on the dockside, pinprick pulse
of respiration; who was once and once was, ounce—
get up, get up, O girl get up; and walk: that I might live.

Some thing should be given her to eate

From the castle roof let the red cock crow.

The technique is generally juxtaposition: Kaz
wi chips an garlic mayo ont bench by GT News;
Taz with wind-dried blesbok biltong, chez Hez
in the Obs magazine; smug, self-satisfied. Here's
a hundred-million road; there, a hundred-billion
railroad, each shanghaied cargo bristling whips,
City deriving futures: Kaz wi chips an garlic mayo
ont bench by GT News; Taz with gilded dik-
dik testes, chez Fez—with Tez and Jez
(he sez)—on Etihad's First Suite™ flatscreen.

*Joy in the presence
of the Angels of God*

Improvisations on Luke XV

Publicanes and sinners

Far I see, scry bees lapping gold
in the crotch of a dunghill dog,
cock-clipped and de-nutted,
pluckèd of tooth, tits dried
to his ribs like scabs on the hide
of a fly-blown roadside mule.
Flesh is the floor for the drones'
lewd waggle dance; out of the eater
comes forth meat, from the meat
of the eater comes sweetness.
Render to Dagon the holy of holies
and share it on your platforms:
anthropocene, her surgeon's cunt,
his live-streamed publick anus.

Murmured, murmured

And they brought vp an euill report of the land vnto the children of Israel, saying, The land through which we haue gone is a land that eateth vp the inhabitants thereof, and all the people that we saw in it are men of a great stature.

The bough of the beech by the ride at Holy Well Wood
hangs over the path like a rafter, a light-fitting,
a banister rail. What witchcraft did I conjure
that long-haired May Day morning, when I cut
and coiled the azure rope, ravelled the fluttering
crime scene tape and scoured the earth for ejaculate?
Woodpecker gunfire, jays launching Katyushas
from dark rhododendrons, the wreck of the Niggers
in flames. Bombweed blows in the roofless tap,
where ghosts sup Sam's from skulls of scabs
and weave carbon neutral wickerwork coffins,
for Steve and Mark and Brian and Tez, Tony,
Jud and Clarrie. Abide with us up Westfield Lane,
to the shaft of the country park pit: where the bugling
Bristol-to-Newcastle train drops them
in Groundwork's regenerate meadow; where once
the winding gear stood like the sons of Anak,
grashopper scrats his unregenerate bombweed song.

'The Niggers' was the nickname of Frickley Colliery Working Men's Club, South Elmsall. The colliery-owned club acquired the name in 1926, when it was the only place in the village that would serve blacklegs during the year long strike. The name was widely used throughout the club's life, although its legitimacy was increasingly challenged, especially in the lead up to and during the second great strike of 1984–1985, when the club became the base for a particularly militant clique of young socialist miners. Frickley Colliery Working Men's Club closed in 1994, one year after the closure of the pit, and was destroyed in an arson attack in the same year.

This man receiueth sinners

From the head of the table the host broke bread
and blessed it. His guests gave thanks and fell on it
like harpies: the toothless ex-con with the teardrop
tattoo who loosed lurchers at Lincolnshire muntjac;
the lamp-eyed smackhead who splintered
Aggie's ribcage; the rat-faced picker who broke
his wife's jaw and melted her face on the hob ring.
Brayden's granny with her welly-top fanny;
Brayden's mam with skin like Spam. And eyes
like Bovril. The bare-arsed bairn treading shite
into the carpet, turds squashed between his toes:
OO E'S A DIRTY LICKLE BUGGER. Grinning
piccaninnies, spawn of Scouse toms and Nigerian
seamen. *Britain for the British, you fucking
black cunts: don't you know we voted BREXIT?*
Chalice coming round, brimming dark wine:
cheers, says the cheese & onion warehouseman
who raped his niece in the static van; *bottoms up*
says his cumshot trouble-and-strife, who sawed off
his dick with a Stanley knife and's locked up in Ashford
serving life. Plenty more where that came from:
Mini-fucking-Maureen/radged in the head/shagged
Peter Sutcliffe/and now she's dead. E-cig Emmerdale
shithouse cleaners. Neets at ASOS. Days at NEXT.
Frank-a-Tank-Rent-a-Tent, XXXXXXL. Beer
guts, halitosis, nits. The North. Jeremy-fucking-Kyle
Walker's Crisps. Laminate floor, laminate floor,
hot-wired quad bike, laminate floor. Shit schools.
Vicky in the Co-op in her onesie and mules, buying
rizlas, lard and Canesten Duo: she stunk of skunk
and spunk, kerplunk. Buckaroo.
They ate and drank and were briefly merry.
Kaz Matthews' corsey edge disco. Decks and leets
and cans you name it. But the cans were drained,
the leets went out and hearts left blind and empty.

They fell to their knees and beseeched him:
Lord, remember uz, when u cum into yr Kingdumb.
From the head of the table he crowbarred the crates,
breaking out AKs and Little Green Books: and each
received his portion: *Tomorrow shall ye be with me*
                                            in Paradise.

Ninety nine in the wildernesse

Johnny Copley took an axe
and gave his bum-chum forty whacks.
When still he heard the bastard whine
he gave him another fifty-nine.

He took off in the ice cream van
to a boarding house in Bridlington
and signed his name in the visitors' book
with the van's bright decal—Donald Duck.

John sauntered down the Promenade
and played the fruits in Mick's Arcade.
He killed time in the Pompadour
sinking pots by the shithouse door.

At last orders the lad turned up
and Johnny shared a loving cup
with his bleached-blonde, borstal boy rough trade—
the bingo caller from Mick's Arcade.

By the bogs they shared a kiss
and smooched to jukebox Johnny Mathis
each clinging tightly to his squeeze
until the bell rang 'time gents please'.

They staggered up the road together,
singing Misty and The Twelfth of Never,
and fumbling for keys at Ocean View
John sighed, I'm stone in love with you.

They creaked the stairs of Johnny's digs,
turned on with poppers and herbal cigs—
then John pulled out his bloody chopper
and gave it to him good and proper.

Johnny woke—or was he dreaming,
cops with cuffs and truncheons screaming—
but Johnny had run out of luck:
they'd traced him through the Donald Duck.

They marched him down the hotel stairs
past gawping guests quite unaware
that Donald from the ice cream van
was Johnny Copley, the mad axeman.

They shoved him in the Black Maria
and cuffed him up behind the wire.
But the Transit never made the clink
cos the alternator was on the blink.

And that's how Johnny ended up
a final time in the Donald Duck
cuffed to the freezer en route to the nick
singing along to the Teddy Bear's Picnic.

Heartened by the way they'd chimed
Johnny begged that one last time
he'd be allowed to park his van
as Donald Duck, the ice cream man.

Three wise monkeys kept them sweet
and they turned off onto Fraisthorpe beach
where Johnny served those three bent coppers
two ninety-nines and a strawberry woppa.

The Judge gave him life like shelling peas,
and recommended no release
for this *homosexual psychopath/
perverted lust/blah-blah/bloodbath*.

John thought the whole thing was a farce
and told him stick it up your arse:
he was well-acquainted with the Judge
from Bell Street bogs, where they both packed fudge.

They banged him up in Wakefield nick
but Johnny didn't take no shit
from the psychos, nonces and sex cases,
serial killers and London faces.

And shortly Johnny took a shiv
and holed some fat poof like a sieve—
because the cockney bastard played
with his bleached-blonde, borstal boy rough trade.

No repentance

The bayonet tip wouldn't bite at first.
Scraped, slid off, like his vest was made
of mithril. Lothlorien, Gonvilnd Keys.
A gift from the Lady, or Arron Banks.
Barings Bank. The plunderous karats
of Antwerpus Loup. The bayonet tip
wunt bite the thick-seamed ephod,
its armour of urin and bummin. Deep
bruzing, dribling facets. Sum wailing:
Paedo/haemo-philiac sadness. Bayonet
tip at bay, tight-mesh kevlar whalebone
corset. Waling. Rifle butt or handy rock
by hand. Cracked crabshell, the bright
blood oh the bright and black bright
blood. Phil Leotardo's pancaked dome:
CROCK. Spill it—dimunz, perlz, Old
English Spangles. Frayed linen tricklin
rubies: names stitched into underpants
unravel—Willum, Judd, Alexey, Blud.
Clubbin ducklins with Garrard & Flack:
that kind of thing, but for the greater good.
Mess up the wall and over the concrete
floor: spatter of sapphires and scattring
blue-tongued skinks. Chromosomes
uncrowned, crowned kids rinsed in blood
as Blood. The boy died at my pleasure,
like a rabbit retrieved to hand or a ball-
bellied Sudanese refugee: eyes glazing
over, ribcage ever so slightly lifting STOP
won't somebody think of the children?

Reioyce

And when hee had opened the fift seale, I saw vnder the altar, the soules of them that were slaine for the word of God, and for the testimony which they held. And they cried with a lowd voice, saying, How long, O Lord, holy and true, doest thou not iudge and auenge our blood on them that dwell on the earth?

The slaughtered of Europe, Garefowl,
Pied Raven and Slender-billed Curlew, crying
for justice and restoration, the Old Earth
and no Heaven, Angels of gibbets and fire.

The Lambe unleashed Kezef to blast the land with phosphor: the cities burned and fell to ash, where spring rain fed the fescues: wolves denned among birches, under vitrified concrete: and the roes that browsed the pavement corn were sleek and knew no fear.

The wasted of Asia, Javan Lapwing,
Spectacled Cormorant and machine-gunned Kharchal,
beating their breasts and praying for pestilence,
that their wasters sicken, their sickened lands bloom waste.

The Lambe sent Af, his raving scythe: for he adored the Earth: from Caucasus to Komandorsk, he reaped them like a dry paddy: their warm blood gushed and fed the kelp: and sea cows rolled like right whales in the cold and weedy deeps.

The annihilate of Africa, Waldrapp, Liben Lark,
Nechisar Nightjar, tearing their feathers in grief
for their snuffed DNA, demanding blood to plume
their bones, asperging Thrones, Dominions.

The Lambe commanded Hemah to slay them in their cradles: his weevils seethed in the barns of Sheba and limed the veldt with bones: where bluebuck leap in tall tambookie, unnumbered herds of twin-dropped quagga roam.

The extinguished of AMERICA, California Condor,
Spix's Macaw, Sierra Madre's Imperial Woodpecker,
howling for vengeance, for their strangled posterities,
their torn and poisoned, bought and broken lands.

> *Terrible MASHHIT He sent, with heroin cut with anthrax, meth*
> *with botulinum: and he fed them white bread, beef and steroids,*
> *and boiled them alive in lead: where the black-footed ferret*
> *and Jamaican rice rat spurt from their unlocked graves.*

Holocaust OCEANIA, Kaua'i 'O 'o, Kakapo, Bourbon
Crested Starling, lamenting their ship-shattered Edens,
where their children were fed to pigs, and bloodlines addled
in the stillborn egg: death becoming, becoming nothing.

> *The Lambe commanded Cruel MESHABBER to rid the plague*
> *from the pimpled seas: and he caused the stars to raze*
> *the streets then raised the rinsing waves: and the devil*
> *and tiger stropped their claws and tore the joyful bandicoot.*

***

The babushkas of Chernobyl chose life
among the wolves. The geiger counter
goes bleep-bleep-bleep-bleep-bleep.
No running water, electricity: brown bear,
bison, boar, red deer; goshawk, Tengmalm's owl.
One day, those old women will be dead;
their sons and daughters, all their kin.
Shacks collapsed and gardens thick with weeds.
Elk shredding his velvet, splintering lintels.
The geiger counter goes BLEEP. BLEEP. BLEEP.
BLEEP. BLEEP. Not with a bang, but a whimper.
WHIMPER. WHIMPER. WHIMPER. WHIMPER. BANG.

Ioy in the presence of the Angels of God

Epigonium aphyllium

Brockadale, a steaming August morning after weeks
of siling rain. Mist hanging beneath the beechwoods,
rising from the swollen river bellied between the trees.
Rumbling traffic from the Great North Road, clanking
plant in the Went Edge quarry; swans and turquoise
haylage floating. Glede aloft over storied Saylis,
where under the nave of vaulting beeches, one rummages
in the leaf litter, his sixth decade of darkwood dreaming,
his sixth decade of grail-less gold; birds-nest, helleborine,
lilac leg; so very close, so—from the canopy comminutus
calling lifts his eyes to the rifting crowns, where a bolt of sun
blinds the wood Damascus, gilding his frame in a shaft of light:
and *there*, bright between his scuffed Doc Martens,
the pallid fungoid spike he'd searched for all his pilgrim life—
here am I, for thou diddest call me. And ermines bloomed
from the ruptured earth and pranced across the loam,
under the thunder of rutting aurochsen, the roaring
throats of bears; and he leapt with the fitches like David.
How long wilt thou be drunken? Put away thy wine from thee.
But I will leap with all my might and glory in my shame:
for when the pale ghost walks in Robenhode's forest
will the armour-plated sturgeon break the waters of the Went,
campephilis trumpet on the Choctawatchee river.

A farre country

… I can picture them right now,
in the woods, going at it like rutting birds,
clutching each other as they make sweet love.

Domenico Balbi's Fool; Dick Whittington and his Cat;
Dionysus and his panther. Set out, get rich, get wasted;
go dogging with the King of Thebes, looked-after White
Supremacist schoolgirls. They'll do it for love, for cigs
and cider. You're living the dream—Tiberius, Gary Glitter.
Then oh no! #MeToo MILFic violence; you're ripped
to shreds like Harvey Weinstein and even gym can't fix it;
the King's cracked mama's got your head on a stick,
dripping gore on the couch next to Piers and Susanna,
celeb philologist Johnny Allegro, sexpert on the Greeks.
Turn again, Whittington. Get back to your potato patch.
These me-me-metropolitan cunts are all on fucking mushrooms.

The huskes that the swine did eate

What makes a Happy Meal® happy?
Fun and toys in every meal: HA-HA
plastic Super Mario, french fries, zebu,
ketchup, salt. Lickle cardboard box
wiv angles, Diznee AnselnGretlouse.
Can *we* have one, Dad? Battenberg
licks his lips. The little fat bastards
are coming on nicely, making progress
in STEM and subcutaneous tenderisation.
They'll burst like ortolans on his tyranno
saur epicure's tongue. The bony claws
of his butcherbird, pinshin plump thighs
through the bars of the cage, cackling
HA!-HA!-HA!-HA!-HA!—garden party
chipolatas, Archer's shepherd's pies.
Bruised and butterfat Bunter's a blurter—
er krownza pointyat!—and off he went
down the Buxted conveyor with the dross
from the Water Closet Academy Trust.
Sat ramrod straight by the belt-end skip,
knives and forks erect: the jolly Johnsons,
gut-bucket Soames, those preening cunts
off Dragon's Den. Each kid they devoured
was specky, autistic or riddled with tumours.
They sucked their cracked marrowbones
and did everything else they reasonably
could. And the bereft fat bastard mummies
and daddies were everso moved and grateful.
Meanwhile, upstate at Celso's pig farm,
K.O. was chumming Bender in the troughs:
and a lightbulb blurted in Bunter's head
and rolled him off the abbatoir belting.
Wot if, he was finking, *all ve lickle pygs
get togevver an kill an eet ve byg pygges.
Ven veedall B Happy®*. He put his lard

into training with K.O. and Pro, a multitude
of white-lipped peccaries. What they left
was Fabergé bridgework, traces of squam
DNA. Fun and toys in every meal.

No man gaue vnto him

I knew this tramp once. His name was Cyril Bruce.
He chased Rommel from Tobruk to El Alamein.
They demobbed him to Kirkby pit, but three years
under the gemméd azure and naked splendour of Nuit
had ruined him for the plummeting cage, the suffocate
dust of parlour curtains. So he festooned himself in filth
and saucepans, tied a string to his dog and went scrumping.
He kipped in the Elmsall brick kilns with Slack Al
and Pongo Hector. And forsooth, the Queen took pity
on him an offered him a crisp. He looked at her gone out.
'Cheese-and-fucking-onion? Stick it up your arse.'
And he clankety-clanked down to Stockingate Spar,
where he stuffed a multipack down his knackers
and legged it for the brickyard, where he feasted on beef,
chicken & bacon and warmed his arse in cooling ash,
bricks that glowed like the wreck of a smouldering Panzer.

I haue sinned against heauen

I stood before the beaks in my corduroy jacket, and pled
my case: that I came in early and went home late, was firm
but fair and empathetic, and marked my books according
to prescription, using only the three permissible inks,
violet, vermilion and crimson lake, each with its specific
purpose and utility, as defined by the Jackpot Academy.
My spreadsheets dazzled with stars and distinctions,
and I fostered orphans and fed the poor with the spare
from my adequate stipend. Thus my charges progressed
into FE and vocational training, securing the means
to their future prosperity, becoming CEOs, popstars
and lawyers. I died in my own arms, the manner preferred
by Michael Gove and Her Majesty's Inspectorate of Schools,
and found myself before the beaks, in my broad wale,
elbow-patched, corduroy jacket, sleeves soaked to the pits
with the blood of the Saints. They flew from the bench
and passed judgement, the wryneck, red-backed shrike
and corncrake, who pecked my name from the book of life
and cast me blind, alone and helpless into the lake of fire.

Fell on his necke

A human being is not a robust construction.
Its nature is to come apart. The neck
seems a particular point of weakness,
every critical thing—spinal cord, jugular,
carotid, trachea—wired through its exposed,
soft-kid pipe-chase. Chopping will get the job done
in a second: sawing takes longer, but not much.
A well-knotted noose and a decent drop
snaps the cervical vertebrae, flopping
the head on a stalk of wilted rhubarb.

A decapitated head looks like the person
it was just a second ago, but gargoyled in the instant.
Neck flesh flaps and eyes stare flat and glassy:
the face shrinks back to a mangelwurzel rictus.
Where does the life go? It is, then it isn't.
The light in the eye, the pulse in the throat,
the bloom on the skin. The fly.

When I saw what Mohammed Emwazi did
to gentle Alan Henning, I vomited my burger
into my lap, a quarter pound of half-digested meat
and cheese. Those heads spiked on the railings
in Raqqa—ketchup, mustard, corrugated pickle—
Mountjoy's lancers, the cabbage fields of Kinsale.
They're not like us—Carew, or Blount, the dashing
Earl of Essex. So pave my vault with horse skulls
that my song might ring from Hell to Earth.
Justice demands that heads should roll. Brass neck
on that! But how else shall we gain Ewtopia?

The fatted calfe

Lush lad with his own car. Money.
McDonalds, Berkeley Red and WKD.
Skunk and coke. Love and attention.
Sex. Sex and violence. Sharing. Smack!

Charismatic teachers. After-school clubs,
praise. As & stars & 9s. 5th percentile.
Fish knives, theatre, wine. Sex and PPE.
London. Money. Happiness. Smack?

I beheld Satan as lightning fall from heauen

An improvisation on Luke X

Exsultet

Behold the handmaid of the Lord: let it be done to me according to your word.

       30th September, 1994—nine months
after New Year's Eve and rumpled sheets
post-Auld Lang Syne. Me shitfaced turning twenty-nine.
You not-so-shitfaced thirty-one. Kids five and two,
the third in the womb three months that March
stopped moving   after I shattered your joy
by proposing you have an abortion: a donkey kick
to the bleating womb, life offered sent bewildered back.
Exult, let them exult, be glad, let earth be glad.
       Briony, Elliot, the dead boy nameless.
But you had a name for him, *our little boy, our baby.*
You don't need to tell me, and you never have.
But you know and I've always known—I wished him dead
and he fled this Herod to Egypt's plunging dark:
where he waits for those who gave him life
and to greet the one that killed him. *Woe vnto thee
Chorazin, wo vnto thee Bethsaida.*
       When I saw your face I wished myself
struck dumb and reft from Earth: but six weeks later
suppressed relief at the news our son was dead
in your womb: that bent you into the grief you bore,
the sadness you bear   alone

The Feather of Ma'at

I have given bread to the hungry and clothed the naked.
I was a husband to the widow and a father to the orphan.

    The womb's a chloride-rusted clock
stopped ticking. The heart's a pillar of salt.
Oh not so, my Lord. Evaporate seas
of foetal urine, foamy jetsam of dead pink shrimp,
licked up by prowling jackals.
                    Sodome going up
like a furnace, the torn-off wing of a lesser flamingo
flung into the dark pleroma, Zoar and what waits there:
rich loam of selfhood's dissolution,
sown with undone chromosomes, warm rain
and the plummeting void. *O let me escape thither,*
(is it not a little one?) and my soule shall liue,
reclining soft on the starry amnion, as angels fall
as fire from heaven and burn out in the night.
    Surely perfect love is felt there, which comes
from perfect understanding. Where sinnes unfetter
and leap to meet annihilating grace: a wretch like me,
scum of the sphynxy earth.
                    Dissolved, they weep
with joy together, the boy, his mother, his sister
and brother: the father freed from outer darkenesse,
still wailing and gnashing his teeth.

The Mother of Naim

Domine, non sum dignus ut intres sub tectum meum:
sed tantum dic verbo et sanabitur anima mea.

  I dreamt I was a surgeon. A woman wept
on the tile of my theatre, cradling her son,
a stainless steel kidney tray of scraped endometrial tissue.
  O, I had compassion, and wished to stay
her weeping—for her sake and for mine.
I dipped my miracle-working hands in blood,
and said, Yong man, Arise.
       And his mother got up.
But her son lay cold in his curettage
and was delivered to HealthCare Environmental,
where the flames of the clinical waste incinerator
leapt like the flames of hell.
       And his father got up.
  Ashes, not sackcloth and ashes: the dust of his death
that cleaveth to me, is wiped off against me.
The glamour of Tyre and Sidon, the exaltation
of Capernaum—fitted kitchen, custom bookshelves,
cars and a social life—he died for me
and freed us for those things.

Tarshish

> *Then Zipporah tooke a sharpe stone, and cut off the foreskinne of her sonne, and cast it at his feete, and said, Surely a bloody husband art thou to mee.*

      The Call—a missed period, a pregnancy test
turned blue—the ecstatic embrace waiting at the threshold
as I stumbled, burdened, out of the stuttering car.
Here am I.
           And there I was, stumbling burdened
from the stuttering car, bushwhacked by the dazzle of your joy:
My heart reioyceth in the LORD, my horne is exalted.
Lust's primaeval telos, conspiracy of DNA
and erogenous innervation. The child, you said,
was a boy child. Speech tangled in my nets.
I stumbled back to the stuttering car and fled.
        The LORD was wrath and sought to smite him dead.
But the thunderbolt missed and struck in the womb
of his wife—O, let not the boy perish for this man's life:
rather cast him into the sea—*they that obserue
lying vanities, forsake their owne mercy.*
        But here I am with my life among the living,
my fleets of ivory, apes and peacocks. A worm in my heart
and a snake beneath my tongue. Elephants strafed
with M16s, baby orang-utans swaddled in diapers:
peacocks crowing on the slopes of Sinjar,
fanning their tails on the grassy mass graves of Yezid.

Ego te absolvo

Assoone as the voice of thy salutation sounded
in mine eares, the babe leapt in my wombe for ioy.

To wish someone dead and fail to kill them
is cowardice and bad faith. Therefore we must be murderers.
The sin is to stay the knife.
      The boy that lit the linnet's nest,
then blubbered over the gaping fledglings
as they writhed in crackling death? There's no forgiveness.
The act can never be undone.
      I was not that boy.
You were a fledgling in the egg. I can't see you,
did not know you—and perhaps that's why I cannot feel
the way I feel I ought.
      I see your mother and fail
to embrace her. I embrace my guilt. I wallow in my guilt.
I go through the motions of wallowing in my guilt.
I try to get a poem out of guilt. I try to get a great poem.
   Guilt is the noblest emotion. It implies
a moral compass, empathy and the love of one's neighbour,
a sense of responsibility. It implies reparations.
It implies I am not worthy of guilt.
      I wish he had been born.
I wish he was twenty-three. I wish I had not hurt
his mother, that she did not know her sadness.
   I wished it. It probably made no difference.
I wish it. It makes no difference.

The Passing of Joel Theriot

You are a stranger to yourself, yet he knows you. And when your hard heart made you like unto the stone and broke you from his body, which is the stars and the wind between the stars, he knew you! He knew you, again and forever. This world is a veil. And the face you wear is not your own.

    Death is a warm dark seed bed.
                                    You lie there
in the moon's soft light. Your ribcage barely rises,
falls; your eyelids droop with pendant sleep.
You smile.
        The stars are uneasy, a ripple
of evening starlings. Blood becoming brine.
The heart's flame flickers.
                          You turn in the loam
and float from the poisoned world.

I beheld Satan as lightning fall from heauen

*Joel Theriot. Yah-is-God the Beast. Jehovah is the Beast.
That's what the cracker preachers know, the tent revivalists:
that their God is a fucking animal.*

When little xy smashed into life on the opening day of the inaugural International Year of Tolerance, his Maker had already planned the Great Hanshin earthquake, the collapse of Barings Banks and Shoko Asahara's sarin attack on the Tokyo Metro, by which time he was almost certainly dead, though not slipped from the womb until the day of the crash of Tarom flight 371 or perhaps the Samashiki massacre. And thus he was spared the despair of sharing the Earth with the bombings in Oklahoma, Navaly and Srebrenica, and the disgrace of sharing his nativity with the prosecution of Guilio Andreotti and the acquittal of O.J. Simpson—the extradition of Eric Priebke, the assassination of Yitzhak Rabin and the enthronement of Gyaincain Norbu as the eleventh Panchen Lama. *BAAA*. Meanwhile, I had a pair of white Valsport Marco Simone Fuoriclasse, an intermittent binge-drinking problem and a tossing yen for Morgan Fairchild lookalike pussy. Plus a lot on my mind, don't forget that—my dreams were dripping with blood and glory. It was about that time I began to judge the world and I taped a machete between my shoulder blades so the hilt popped up beneath the collar. In the heat of debate, I'd reach back, get a grip and start swinging. Thus I removed the servant's ear and made a collateral mess of my friends and family, but barely a scratch on the Tories. God's a cunt and He doesn't exist. I read it in the Morning Star. *In nomine filii et patris et spiritus sancti. Shantih shantih shantih. BAAA-men.*

A Dog Speculates on the Mind of Newton

Human consciousness is a tragic misstep in evolution. We became too self-aware. Nature created an aspect separated from itself—we are creatures that should not exist by natural law. We are things that labor under the illusion of having a self. This accretion of sensory experience and feeling—programed, with total assurance, so that we think we're each somebody, when, in fact, everybody's nobody. I think the honorable thing for our species to do is deny our programing. Stop reproducing. Walk hand-in-hand into extinction.

    The two I know. The one I didn't, that died
before he lived.
        The unknown fruits of the plastic cup—
Emek Clinic, 83, twenty-five shekels a pop.
Various knee tremblers, one-night-stands.
    Haploid waste, the tits of johnnies and spermicidal
diaphragms, coitus interruptus and wanking:
the bloody wastes of womb.
        The trillionfold spores
of calvatia gigantea howl on the solar wind.
What is it that wants to be born so badly?
The selfish gene, working its blind, biochemical magic
via tingly engorgement and dopamine release.
What is it in the cell craves pleasure so badly,
like slugs death-bent on henbane?
        Nothing
begat physics   begat chemistry   begat biology
begat consciousness   begat self-consciousness
begat   physics and chemistry and biology
and consciousness and self-consciousness and
    Nothing.
        The four fundamental forces:
the quintessential fifth—a dark matter.
    The haploid cell, a cold spark of soul
awaiting ignition; the diploid cell, the lit pleroma.
If two survive, we all survive, though all the rest
be dead. Just one and you'd better be Doctor Yakub,

resurrecting the dead with a Frankenstein cocktail
of razorbill ova and musty garefowl DNA.
    On the sixteenth day the larval blastula
reduces to soup and reforms as gastrula's pinhead imago:
organogenesis, SPUC's thumb-sucking Kadmon
of forty solemnised days and nights, when billions
are dumped from the menstrual stink-pit,
that maggoty maelstrom of pointless matter
and bottomless pointless pain. Dawkinsian dope
of awe and wonder can't numb us to the horror.
Bold Irenaeus or Rustin Cohle, the formless
whistling void. The rest is disingenuous love,
the chalk-voiced wolf in the flesh of the trusting lamb.
    Where do our lives go when they exit from this world?
I leapt from the cliff to find out: and emerged
from Carcosa's whirling vortex to Fenwick's
tunnel of light—Clarrie laughing and waving
at the garden gate, cradling his unborn grandson;
Neil grinning and squealing and leaping at the fence,
tail pumping like a piston. The chuckling murmur
of the infinite mown-down dead. *Welcome home.*
Weeping, we embrace each other, the dog up-jumping
and licking my face, the boy-child gazing up
and smiling—*Father, I forgive you*—cheesy effects,
sentimental narrative balm for the hopeless,
sick and grieving.
    Let each one hope and believe what he can.

Goe, and doe thou likewise

Compassion is the vice of kings: stamp down the wretched and the weak: this is the law of the strong: this is our law and the joy of the world.

Loads the Budget van in darkness.
Snarls the track from Coal Pit Farm. White knuckles
on the steering wheel, eyes opalescent in the glaze.
Fly crawling in the ear's pink shrimp. Tinnitus
of wailing babies, the sob of torn foxes.
      Cut engine at the layby junction, the shadow
of Cath's Diner. Dull glow of low-pressure sodium
road lights. Intermittent headlamp blare
on the mud-slicked 638. Air-con drone
from the business park, gulls pealing from the landfill.
Cab pumped with acrid methane. A robin's
mournful whistling in the dark.
      Budget van lights up and snarls to life.
Full beam ectoplasmic barn owl, rats flash
across the camber. Polythene ghosts in rusted hawthorns,
ditch litter of KFC. Tarmac thrums in citrine darkness.
      Service track for the Doncaster-Wakefield
railway line. Chained gate at the stone dump
turning circle—granite ballast, concrete sleepers—
plasterboard and builder's rubble, johnnies
and jamrags, KFC.
      Dawn undimming darkness. Kill the lights,
clunk-click the driver's door. Rumble of distant
landfill lorries, gull tornado whirl and screaming.
Side door scraped open. Redbreast's tick-tick-
tick-tick-ticking—wheel-spin, spurting gravel.
      Darkness lifted, sodium streetlights cold.
White noise from the 638. Walking the dog,
hand raised to his opened mouth—ditch litter of nonces,
wrists cable-tied behind their backs, eyes popped
from broken sockets. Thirty brace of dumped pheasants,

a gargoyled fox in a Tesco bag-for-life.
      Sirens gaining, squalling gulls. Squeal
of brakes, car doors flung open. Crunching boots
in potholed gravel. Robins explode and blackbirds
shatter—ditch litter of blood-soaked Tattershall shirts
and torched Izuzu Troopers—*O my God,*
I am heartily sorry for having offended you
and I detest all my sins, because I dread the loss
of heaven and the pains of hell becoming a grim blur,
because I know I'd do it all again and feel nothing
but—
      The robin's plaint. A magpie's ratchet.
The yellow-eyed glare of a greater black-backed gull.
Toothbrush shivs, tape-handled shards
of carefully broken jam jars. The biohazard
sharp bin. Sid Cooke, Tim Bonner, Beverley Allitt
and me. Life without—full term.
      All this is foul smell and blood in a bag.

Ecce Homo

How should I not be grateful to my whole life?

A naked shrimp, bloody with weals,
crowned in thorns and weeping smiles. Wise as a hoopoe
in its shithole in the orchard.
                        Clever as the mid-term
medical student, swotting for his test: after-cleavage
comes-the-blastula-the-blastula-the-gastrula-ORGANO-
GENESIS—
          Excellent books—nice font,
flattering blurbs from friends and family, underwritten
by hired professionals.
                Why am I a Destiny?
I became what I am. That's how a man becomes what he is.

Capernaum

And thou Capernaum, which art exalted to heauen,
shalt be thrust downe to hell.

    I stood before the Emerald Throne
and asserted my position, that although I had killed
a sparrow, fucked a bespectacled teaching assistant
and wished death on an unborn child,
I had saved a toad's life, formed the committee
that rescued the Common and given one-hundred-
and-fifty pounds to Smile Train. And as for the other things,
I was always heartily sorry.
                    And He said,
Your merits are more contemptible than your sins
and your sorrow is self-pity. The angels lowered
their carbines.
           But He stayed their hands,
saying, I will not be complicit in the contagion
of his darkness.
              Examine your heart and know
what you are: a beast and a murderer. You cannot
be redeemed. Embrace the horror and kill yourself.
In the instant of death, you'll know you've done
the one right thing—let that be your consolation.

Melencolia, I

John came fleeing to the Mother of God, and said to her:
Have you not heard? The Jews have laid hold of my Master,
and are taking Him away to crucify Him—

The artist's mother as frog or precinct baghead.
Bug-eyed with the strain of eighteen labours
that sucked her out like cancer—fifteen swaddled
in the sexton's cradle, three quick boys with hair like girls.
The red one took after his father; the black,
the king of Poland; the Golden Boy with wanderjahre,
Mantegna and Bellini—begging forgiveness
at the tombs of the martyrs, cock deep up Willibald's arse.
Switch-hitter Willibald, riding Agnes to the grave:
he couldn't allow it; her womb had to rattle
like kreuzers in a cup. Venetian courtesans,
or tossing in front of the looking glass, in tasselled caps,
twiddling thistles, in furs, as dreadlocked Jesus Christ.
Hylomorphic polyhedron, fouled perspective and proportion;
all bats and black gall. Goggle-eyed Anne, looming over
the immaculate virgin and child—*fucking Agnes! Just*
like his mother!—suckling her son at the foot of the cross,
stripped and skewered and nailed and torn and bleeding.

—Hearing this, she cried out with a loud voice, saying: Where is my
son? And she rose up, and went along the road weeping. And when they
arrived at the Praetorium, John said: Seest thou Him bearing the crown
of thorns, and having His hands bound? And the Mother of God, hearing
this, and seeing Him, fainted, and fell backwards to the ground, and lay
there a considerable time. And the women, as many as followed her, stood
round her, and wept. And as soon as she revived and rose up, she cried out
with a loud voice: My son, where has the beauty of thy form sunk? How
shall I endure to see thee suffering such things?

Hæc nox est

*Fireflies illumined the darkness, and lightning flashed
on the horizon. But there was no thunder. A weird circular
light glowed in the sky for a few moments and then suddenly
plummeted toward the horizon, a crimson tail behind it.*

  I stepped from the cliff into ocean's
up-thrust, and plummeted in the darkness.
Clap-rattling gannets leapt from the crag and circled
their crosses. Auks dropped from their cracks
and exploded. Fulmars squirting vomit. I flapped
like an oily eagle, and fell.
  Below, the heaving sea, its ghostly freight
of fallen stars and shoals of glittering sturgeon.
Above, the all-enveloping night, the pulsar static
of the empyrean—face peppered with salt-shot,
breath torn-off by up-flung bolts of foam.
  They say the shock of the fall alone
will stun the head and stop the beaten heart;
else splat on the glass of the marbled sea,
and nothing in that instant. But I just kept falling,
a rope-less bucket, dropped in a bottomless well.
  And I thought, perhaps this is it, the way
DMT seeks to ease our deaths in the moment
of transition, that we fall forever, and forever
are spared the shattering shock of impact—
unlike those nights we hit the rocks, and scream
erect in freezing sweat *thank God it's just a dream.*
  It is no dream. The cormorant's embrace
awaits, this flick-book life of a thousand ripped off
guillemot wings, each plucked from the body
and cast to the mantling dark, where this one falls
and continues his falling, a feather of flame
now falling beside him, a small cool flare
of feathery flame, lighting his darkness
and feathering his falling; and now he himself

is transfigured to flame, falling beside the spark
that found him, and together they fall, a flaming man
and a flaming child, with angels, falling,
feathers of flame come flaring from darkness,
like sparks from a rocket or the tail of a comet,
falling together and joining the fallen,
the sobbing father and weeping mother and all
their gathered children, now falling as a single flame,
a single tear of feathery fire, like a flare
from a foundering trawler, dropping bright
in the salt and whistling night, and settling
on the heave like a lotus, or a burning swan,
drifting out on the darkness and sinking.

Notes

The poems in this book are improvisations arising from contemplative readings of four chapters of the 1611 edition of the King James Bible—Matthew VI, Mark V, Luke XV and Luke X. *Lectio Violant*—'profane reading'—is the name I've coined to describe this process, alluding to *Lectio Divina*—'divine reading'—the long-established Catholic practice of devotional reading, the purpose of which is to draw the reader closer to God by enabling a fuller experience of scripture. I'm not sure this book's doing the same thing, although you never know.

Lectio Violant is an impossible compound in Latin, although Google Translate will tell you otherwise. *Lectio Violenta* is the preferred play on *Lectio Divina*. But the wilful perversity of *Lectio Violant* enacts the method and embodies the content and is thus preferred.

Sufficient vnto the day
Improvisations on Matthew VI

Treasures of heaven and earth: all the species that can be identified with certainty from Albrecht Dürer's 1503 watercolour *'Das große Rasenstück'* ('The Large Piece of Turf') were used in Dürer's time as treatments for venereal diseases or other maladies of the genito-urinary tract. 'Wick' is a Yorkshire dialect word meaning 'infested with'. **Theeues breake thorow:** the epigraph is from Aleister Crowley's *The Book of the Law*. **Where your treasure is, there will your heart be also:** the various pearmains, ribstons, burrknots, ploughmen, catsheads and Nancy Jacksons are cultivars of the apple. The epigraph is taken from Bridget Gillespie's description of the Nancy Jackson, quoted in Linden Hawthorne's superb *The Northern Pomona: Apples for Cool Climates* (2007). **How great is that darkenesse:** the 'macula' is that part of the retina which enables the eye to focus sharply. **No man can serve two masters:** 'pagurus' is the edible crab. **Take no thought for your life:** in 1969 'Charlie' Manson made his headquarters at the 'Spahn movie ranch'. 'Tex' was Manson's follower, Charles Watson. 'L. Ron Hubbard' founded Scientology. **The foules of the aire:** 'Drax' is a Yorkshire power station that burns 'biomass'—wooden pellets made from clear-felled American forests. Nightjars nesting nearby hunt moths under the power station floodlights. **The lillies of the field:** '*fumaria officinalis*' is the common fumitory, the preferred food of the turtle dove. A once common species in England and Wales, the turtle dove has declined catastrophically since the 1970s and seems likely to go extinct here within the next decade or so. Turtle doves were offered as sin offerings in the Jerusalem temple. **Solomon in all his glory:** 'Shirebrook' in Derbyshire is the non-union, zero-hour contract, minimum wage heart of billionaire Mike Ashley's *Sports Direct* empire. In 2016 'Sting' accepted a million dollars from Russian oligarch Said Gutseriev to do a turn at his daughter's wedding. **Yee of little faith:** 'pratensis' is the meadow pipit, 'perdix' is the grey partridge, 'sambucus' is the elder, 'jynx' is the wryneck and the italic lines are from *Piers Plowman*. **The kingdome of God, and his righteousnesse:** the epigraph is courtesy of Jennifer Melfi in the *The Sopranos* ('Cold Cuts', season five, episode ten). **Sufficient vnto the day is the euill thereof:** the 'pern' is the honey buzzard. 'Arcturus' alludes to David Lindsay's book, *A Voyage to Arcturus* (1920). 'Yuggoth' is the home of Great Cthulhu in a number of stories by H.P. Lovecraft, including *The Call of Cthulhu and Other Weird Stories* (2002).

The countrey of the Gadarenes
Improvisations on Mark V

The countrey of the Gadarenes: 'DMT' is N,N-Dimethyltryptamine, a substance that occurs naturally in many plants and animals and which can also be artificially synthesised. It is used for ritual and entheogenic purposes in many cultures. **No man could bind them:** 'Ben Dyker' was the main character of the BBC children's TV show *Striker* (1975–6). **Jesus afarre off:** 'Trampas' was a lurcher. The epigraph is from I Corinthians XVI: 22. **A great herd of swine, feeding:** the garefowl is extinct and the 'glaucous macaw' and 'slender-billed curlew' are probably so, all three as a result of human activity. The 'jenny wren' is not extinct and may well be the most common species of bird in Europe, just as the 'passenger pigeon' was once the most numerous species of bird on the planet. President Harry 'Truman' dropped two atomic bombs on Japan. 'Djugashvili' is Josef Stalin. **Publish in Decapolis:** Camillo 'Torres' was a revolutionary

Colombian priest who was killed in combat in 1966. 'Dedan Kimathi' was a Kenyan revolutionary leader executed by the British in 1957. 'Tudiya' is the first name on the Assyrian King List. 'Under their skirts' references the sicarii, a zealot group in first century Palestine, who would conceal daggers in their clothing which they used opportunistically to cut the throats of their Roman oppressors. **All men did marueille:** 'Kahless' is the Klingon Messiah in *Star Trek*. 'Anthony Robbins' is a celebrity U.S. motivational speaker. **Had suffered many things, of many Physicians:** the 'maingate rip' is a term from coal-mining. The maingate was one of two roadways to the face (the other being the tailgate). A ripper removed the rock from above the seam at the coal-face. 'Chocks' were wooden or hydraulic devices used to prop up the roof of the face. **Be not afraid, onley believe:** 'belendek' and 'dwale' are the Old English names for henbane and deadly nightshade, respectively; 'datura' is the thornapple. Ravenser Odd was a coastal town near what is now Spurn Point. 'Cockayne' is the mythical land of plenty in the European peasant tradition. In Hinduism, and subsequently Anthroposophy, the 'Akashic record' is a kind of spiritual master-recording of everything that has ever happened in time and space, accessible to adepts. The epigraph is taken from W.H. Murray's *The Scottish Himalayan Expedition* (1951). **Why make ye this adoe, and weepe?:** 'Liz Blakelock's' husband Keith was hacked to death by a mob during the Broadwater Farm riots of 1986. 'Winnie' Silcock spent over a decade in prison, wrongly convicted of the murder. Lord 'Denning' convicted six innocent Irishmen of the Birmingham pub bombings. 'Karen Matthews' staged the kidnapping of her daughter Shannon in 2008 so she could claim the reward money when Shannon was 'rediscovered'. Clarence 'Odbody' is the angel who talks George Bailey out of committing suicide in *It's a Wonderful Life*. The epigraph is from Thomas Jefferson's letter to William Smith (13th November, 1787), commenting on 'Shay's Rebellion', an insurrection of Massachusetts farmers. **The damosell is not dead, but sleepeth:** this poem is a meditation on the ruin of St. Helen's Chapel, near Barnburgh, South Yorkshire. Fieldwork undertaken in 2011 by the University of Sheffield's Department of Archaeology demonstrated continuity of ritual activity in the area of the chapel ruin—once the site of a sacred spring and latterly a holy well—from the Mesolithic to the Early Modern period. The chapel was founded in the twelfth century and seems to have become a cult-centre or pilgrimage site, its stonework being decorated with royal and baronial coats-of-arms, and an extensive graveyard testifies to the fact that many sought to be buried there. The chapel was destroyed during the Tudor expropriation of the English Catholic church. 'Alice & Percy' are Alice & Percival Cresacre, Lady and Lord of the Manor of Barnburgh in the fifteenth century. **Some thing should be given her to eate:** Karen Matthews, Tara Palmer Tompkinson, Heston Blumenthal, Ferran Adrià, Teresa May and Jeremy Corbyn are abbreviated. Mark E. Smith's characterisation of the *Observer* Magazine in 'How I wrote 'Elastic Man" (1980) is paraphrased in the fourth line. The epigraph is taken from an English translation of a German revolutionary song, 'The Black Band of Florian Geyer'.

Ioy in the presence of the Angels of God
Improvisations on Luke XV

Publicanes and sinners: the story of Samson in Judges XIII-XVI is alluded to. **Murmured, murmured:** Frickley Colliery was the pit at the top of 'Westfield Lane'. The epigraph is from Numbers XIII: 32. **This man receiueth sinners:** 'grinning piccaninnies' is borrowed from Enoch Powell, and his disingenuous plagiarist, Boris Johnson. 'Spawn of Scouse toms and Nigerian seamen' is a paraphrase of former Merseyside Chief Constable Kenneth Oxford's 1981 characterisation of the inhabitants of Toxteth. 'Kaz Matthew's corsey edge disco' took place on the street outside the eponymous Kaz's house when her 'abducted' daughter Shannon was 'discovered' alive and well. **Ninety nine in the wilderness:** this poem is a reimagining of a murder that took place in South Kirkby during the late 1960s or early 1970s. **No repentance:** this poem begins in the cellar at the Ipatiev House, Yekaterinburg on 17th July, 1918, and the difficulty the Bolsheviks had in executing the Russian royal family because the jewellery sewn into their underwear deflected both bullets and bayonets. 'Phil Leotardo' was a character from *The Sopranos* whose head was crushed under the wheel of a Ford Escape (*Made in America*, season six, episode twenty-one). 'Willum', 'Judd' and 'Alexey' are royal princes. 'Garrard & Flack' make posh cricket bats. **Reioyce:** all the bird (and animal) species listed are either extinct or critically endangered.

The capitalised proper names in the italic verses are those of the Five Archangels of Punishment listed by Adolph Jellinek in *Beth ha-Midrasch* (1938). The exclusion zone around the former Soviet nuclear power station at 'Chernobyl' has rewilded in the absence of human activity. However, a number of older women, dissatisfied with their lives in the towns to which they were relocated, have returned to their cottages and eke out a living from their radioactive plots. The epigraph is from the Revelation of S. John the Diuine, VI: 9-10. **Ioy in the presence of the Angels of God:** 'Epigonium aphyllium' is the Ghost Orchid, England's rarest and most elusive flower. The poem is set in the beechwood at Saylis, above the river Went, in Robin Hood's Barnsdale. A 'glede' is a red kite. 'Comminutus' is the lesser-spotted woodpecker. David 'leapt' and danced with joy in II Samuel VI: 14-22, much to his wife Michal's displeasure. The fifth line from the end of the poem is Eli's dismissive comment to his wife Hannah in I Samuel I: 14. He thought she was drunk, but she was talking to God. 'Here am I, for thou diddest call me' is Samuel's exemplary response to God's call in I Samuel III: 5. 'Campephilis' is the almost certainly extinct ivory-billed woodpecker, which some nevertheless believe might be hanging on in the catchment of Florida's 'Choctawatchee river'. **A farre country:** the Spanish artist 'Domenico Balbi' designed a famous Tarot pack; the iconographies of the 'Fool', 'Dick Whittington' and 'Dionysus' share many affinities. Biblical scholar 'Johnny Allegro' wrote *The Sacred Mushroom and the Cross* (1970), in which he argued that Christianity developed under the influence of mystical experiences engendered by the consumption of hallucinogenic mushrooms. The epigraph is from *The Bacchae*, 1180-82. **The huskes that the swine did eate:** 'Battenburg' is a male member of the British Royal Family. STEM is Science, Technology, Engineering & Mathematics, the only subjects deemed worthy of study in England's state education system. Jeffrey Archer served 'shepherd's pie' at the champagne receptions he held when he was Tory Party chairman. Frank Richard's venal and gluttonous schoolboy anti-hero Billy 'Bunter' seems to be the hero of this piece. Joe 'Celso' was a New York mobster who owned a pig farm that his mafia associates would use to dispose of the corpses of their victims—Harold 'K.O.' Konigsberg fed Anthony 'Tony Bender' Strollo to the pigs there. 'Pro' is Tony Provenzano, one of the mobsters involved in the disappearance of Jimmy Hoffa. 'White-lipped peccaries' have been known to devour human beings. 'Squam'—

from squamata, the genus to which lizards belong. **No man gaue vnto him:** 'the gemmed azure and naked splendour of Nuit' is appropriated from *The Book of the Law*. A 'Panzer' is an Armoured Face Conveyor, a German-built machine formerly used in British pits to transport coal away from the face. **Fell on his necke:** 'Mohamed Emwazi' is the Islamist sociopath 'Jihadi John'. 'Alan Henning' is the Manchester taxi-driver turned aid worker whose head Emwazi sawed off on video. Emwazi's fellow sociopaths Charles 'Blount', (Lord Mountjoy, the 1st Earl of Devonshire), Sir George 'Carew' and Robert Devereux, the 'Earl of Essex' lopped many heads in the campaign against Hugh O'Neill's forces in Ireland. O'Neill lopped a few as well, realising that in order to achieve his 22 Articles (regarded by Sir Robert Cecil as 'Ewtopia') heads would have to roll.

I beheld Satan as lightning fall from heaven
An improvisation on Luke X

Exsultet: in the Western Catholic tradition, the *Exsultet* is a proclamation sung before the Paschal candle during the Easter Vigil. The epigraph is Marie's obedient response to the Angel Gabriel in Luke I: 38. **The Feather of Ma'at:** Ma'at was the Egyptian goddess of justice who weighed the heart of the deceased against a feather. A sinful heart was heavier than the feather and was devoured by the demon Ammit. A pure heart was lighter than the feather and its owner was able to join Osiris in the afterlife. The epigraph is from an ancient Egyptian tomb inscription listed in James P. Allen's *Middle Egyptian: An Introduction to the Language and Culture of Hieroglyphs* (2000). The italic phrases embedded in the poem are from Genesis XIX, 'Zoar' being the city God provided as a refuge for Lot during His obliteration of Sodome and Gomorrah. The 'pleroma' (Greek: 'fullness') is the gnostic godhead, comprising the totality of spirit in the universe, symbolised as a single flame. Individual souls incarnate in matter are merely separated-off sparks of the pleroma and each one yearns to return to the comfort, bliss and plenitude of its origin. **The Mother of Naim:** Jesus brought the sonne of the 'Mother of Naim' back from the dead in Luke VII—'Yong man, Arise.' The Latin epigraph is taken from the liturgy of the Mass and is based on the story of the healing of the Centurion's servant, also in Luke IV. **Tarshish:** in the book of Jonah the eponymous hero responds to his 'Call' not with the programmatic obedience—'Here am I'—of Samuel, Isaiah, Elijah or Marie, but by attempting to duck his mission by fleeing to Tarshish. The italic quote beginning, 'they that obserue …' is from Jonah II: 8; 'My heart reioyceth in the Lord, my horne is exalted' was Hannah's ecstatic response to her discovery that she was pregnant in I Samuel II: 1. The 'LORD' sought to kill Moses in Exodus IV: 24, an intention thwarted by his wife Zipporah in the act narrated in the succeeding verse, appropriated for the poem's epigraph. King Solomon controlled the fleets of Tarshish that brought him 'ivory, apes and peacocks' (I Kings X: 22). Sinjar is a largely Yezidi town in Nineveh province, Iraq, the site of genocidal massacres of Yezidis by Daesh in 2014. The Yezidis worship God, or perhaps Lucifer, in the form of Melek Ta'us, 'The Peacock Angel-King'. **Ego te absolvo:** the title is the phrase uttered by the priest at the climax of the ritual of the Catholic sacrament of Reconciliation. The epigraph is from Luke I: 41. **The Passing of Joel Theriot:** Joel Theriot is an evangelical preacher played by Shea Whigham in Nic Pizzolatto & Cary Joji Fukunaga's *True Detective* (2014). The epigraph is an extract from his sermon in episode three, 'The Locked Room'. **I beheld Satan as lightning fall from heaven:** Talmudic tradition, reflected in Luke X:18, asserts that lightning is the 'crack between the worlds' and that each time it flashes, a demon (that is, a fallen angel) descends to earth. All the events referred in the poem took place in 1995. **A Dog Speculates on the Mind of Newton:** the title comes from a line in a letter from Charles Darwin to Asa Gray, dated 22 May 1860, in which he asserts his tentative Deist belief that the universe is the result of intelligent design left to develop according to chance. Darwin eventually concludes that the matter of ultimate origins is too profound for the human mind—'a dog might as well speculate on the mind of Newton'. The concluding line of the poem is a direct quote from the letter. The poem's epigraph is another quotation from *True Detective*— this time from detective Rustin Cohle in episode one, 'The Long, Bright Dark'. 'The Emek clinic' is a fertility centre near Afula, Israel. 'Calvatia gigantea' is the giant puffball. 'Doctor Yakub' is the mad scientist figure who created the evil white race in a laboratory experiment, according to the teachings of the Nation of Islam. 'Kadmon' is Adam Kadmon, the primordial man in Kabbalistic tradition, a being of pure spirit and infinite potential. 'Irenaeus' argued that God deliberately designed a world in which evil and suffering exist, because otherwise it would not be possible for humans to exercise their free will or experience the challenges and consequences that enable development beyond a state of infantile dependency. 'Carcosa' is the barbaric cult developed under the protection of the powerful Tuttle family in *True Detective*. Peter 'Fenwick' was a British neuroscientist who researched Near Death Experiences. **Goe, and do thou likewise:** the epigraph is another quotation from *The Book of the Law*. The italic quotation towards the end of the poem is from the Act of Contrition. 'Sid Cooke' is a notorious paedophile and child-murderer, currently incarcerated at H.M.P. Wakefield. 'Tim Bonner' is Director of the Countryside Alliance. 'Beverley Allitt' is a paediatric nurse from Grantham who killed several of the children in her care. She is currently detained at Rampton Secure Hospital. The final line is from Marcus Aurelius's *Meditations*. **Ecce Homo:** the title is taken from Nietzsche's book of the same name, which is also the source of the epigraph. 'Ecce Homo' ('Behold the Man') are Pilate's words on being presented with Jesus in the Vulgate version of John XIX: 5. **Capernaum:** 'Smile Train' is a charity that works in the developing world to provide reconstructive surgery for children with cleft palates. **Melencolia, I:** 'Melencolia 1' is a 1514 engraving by Albrecht Dürer. The poem alludes to many aspects of Dürer's work and life—his portrait of his mother Barbara; his trips to Italy; his paintings of Saint Jerome; his wealthy and sybaritic friend & patron, Willibald Pirckheimer; his attitude to his wife, Agnes, and his narcissism. The epigraph is from a late version of the apocryphal *Gospel of Nicodemus,* which is the source of the vignette later developed by the Church into the devotional trope that became known as the 'Swoon of the Virgin'. Dürer alludes to the 'swoon' in his 'Lamentation of Christ' (1500) and in his 'Seven Sorrows of the Virgin' (1496-98). **Hæc nox est:** 'This is the night', a refrain from the *Exsultet*. The epigraph is taken from Isaac Bashevis Singer's story, 'The Gentleman from Cracow' (*Collected Stories*, 1982).